WELCOME

To the Student

Piano Fun for Adult Beginners is designed as an entree into the world of Recreational Music Making (RMM). Although you will learn to read music, play music of your choice and learn to play lead sheets, you are starting down a path of music making designed to be stress free and enjoyable.

RMM learning is considered a "dream-fulfillment" opportunity. Countless adults have yearned to play the piano for years (or regretted quitting as a child), and they are seeking a learning environment that helps them achieve that dream. Seize this opportunity and remember, there is no expiration date on dreams.

Audio is included with this book. Each song has two accompaniment tracks. The first is recorded slower as a practice tempo. The second track number is slightly faster. All accompaniments begin with an introduction.

There's a myth that you must have talent to play music. Actually you only need persistence. Remember that diligent practice develops skill. Anyone who wants to play the piano will play the piano. *Piano Fun for Adult Beginners* is a partner in this endeavor. Welcome and enjoy!

To the Teacher

Recreational Music Making piano teachers are a special breed. They understand that RMM students want to learn how to read music and play piano in a relaxed atmosphere with the emphasis on student goals rather than teacher goals. RMM teachers have a unique opportunity to partner with adults who are fulfilling their dreams.

Piano Fun for Adult Beginners is based on music fundamentals or concepts that help students learn to read music and to play music of their choice. Examples of these fundamentals include keyboard geography, music alphabet, rhythm, counting, grand staff, directional reading, chords and lead sheets, and major and minor triads.

Although *Piano Fun for Adult Beginners* can be taught to an individual, it has proven to be especially successful with groups. The size of the group depends on the teacher's comfort level. If adults enroll for eight week sessions, this book is recommended for two eight-week enrollments (sixteen weeks). Some classes may finish it sooner and some may take longer.

Teachers who create a relaxed environment for both the students and themselves will succeed at this endeavor. If you haven't experienced it before, you will soon realize that a non-stressful environment for the student can be the same for the teacher. Welcome and enjoy!

For more information about RMM teaching, the Appendix includes ten frequently-asked-questions on pp. 67–69.

TABLE OF CONTENTS

PIANO FUN
FOR ADULT BEGINNERS

Recreational Music Making
for Private or Group Instruction

Modules by Brenda Dillon

Accompaniments by Ric Iannone

To access audio visit:
www.halleonard.com/mylibrary
Enter Code
2116-4905-3626-6411

ISBN 978-1-4234-8989-4

HAL•LEONARD®
7777 W. BLUEMOUND RD. P.O. BOX 13819 MILWAUKEE, WI 53213

Visit Hal Leonard Online at
www.halleonard.com

ACKNOWLEDGEMENTS

For me, the most rewarding aspect of any endeavor is working with a team of individuals who are dedicated to the best possible outcome. Jennifer Linn's superb editing skills kept raising the bar while continuing to make the project enjoyable and fulfilling. Ric Iannone's creative accompaniments added sounds that allow beginners to play along with more complex textures. Don Dillon (my husband) was constantly encouraging and his software skills produced a daily visual representation that made this book far easier to accomplish. I am genuinely grateful to this team.

—Brenda Dillon

MODULE 1
KEYBOARD GEOGRAPHY

KEYBOARD GEOGRAPHY

Keyboard geography helps to understand and describe a location. The keyboard has a geography of white and black keys. Play keys to the right and the sound is higher. Play keys to the left and the sound is lower.

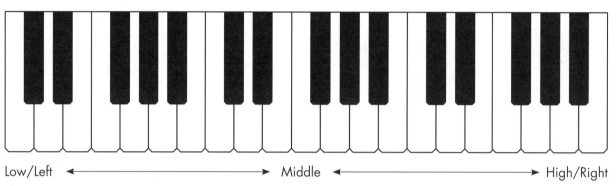

Low/Left ← → Middle ← → High/Right

BLACK KEY CLUSTERS

The black piano keys are arranged in clusters of two's and three's.

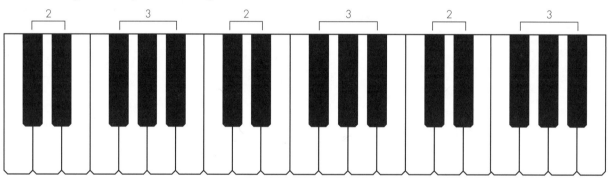

FINGER NUMBERS

Finger numbers on both hands are the same. Thumbs are 1, pointer fingers are 2, middle fingers are 3, ring fingers are 4 and little fingers are 5. Wiggle each finger and name it.

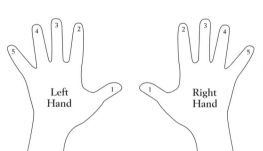

SITTING POSITION

Sit tall, lean slightly forward, keep feet flat on the floor, relax shoulders, place hands on piano and keep forearms level with the keyboard.

PREPARE

1. Place your right hand RH thumb on the lower of two black keys and your little finger on the highest of three black keys. The other fingers play the black keys in between.

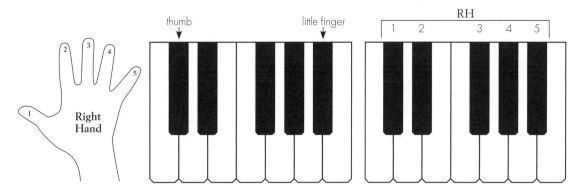

2. Say the word "hold" the number of times indicated.

3. Remember to repeat.

4. Each song has two accompaniment tracks. The first is recorded slower as a practice tempo. The second track number is slightly faster. Both tracks begin with an introduction.

PLAY

TRACKS
1/2

Rainy Days and Black Keys

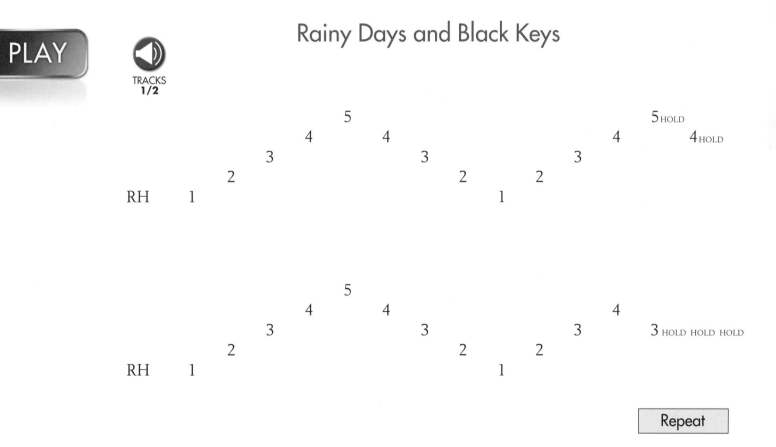

Repeat

HAND POSITION

Curve your fingers when you play, with the
thumb on its side.

PREPARE

1. Place left hand LH fingers (3 2) on a cluster of two black keys. Place right hand RH fingers (2 3 4) on a cluster of three black keys.

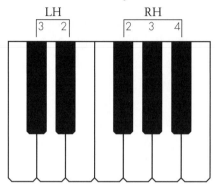

2. After hearing the introduction on track 3, sing the words (or hum the melody) and play the black key patterns as indicated below.

PLAY

🔊 TRACKS **3/4**

Water Is Wide

Traditional

	Left Hand	Right Hand

The water is wide_____

    3 2 3   2   3

I cannot get o-er_____

    4 3 2   3   4

And neither have I_____

    4 3 2   3   4

Wings to fly_____

    3 2 3   2   3

Give me a boat_____   4 3 2 3 4

That can carry two_____   3 2 3 2 3

And both shall row_____   4 3 2 3 4

My love and I._____   3 2   2 2

I leaned my back_____   3 2 3 2 3

Up against an oak_____   4 3 2 3 4

I thought it was_____   4 3 2 3 4

A trusty tree_____   3 2 3 2 3

But first it bent_____   4 3 2 3 4

And then it broke_____   3 2 3 2 3

Just as my love_____   4 3 2 3 4

Was false to me._____   3 2   2 2

9

PREPARE

1. Place your RH five fingers on the same black piano keys you played on *Rainy Days and Black Keys*.

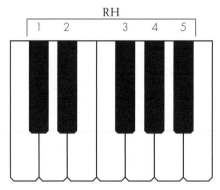

2. Say the word "hold" the number of times indicated.

PLAY

x

x

x

Jolly Old St. Nicholas

Traditional 19th Century
American Carol

TRACKS
5/6

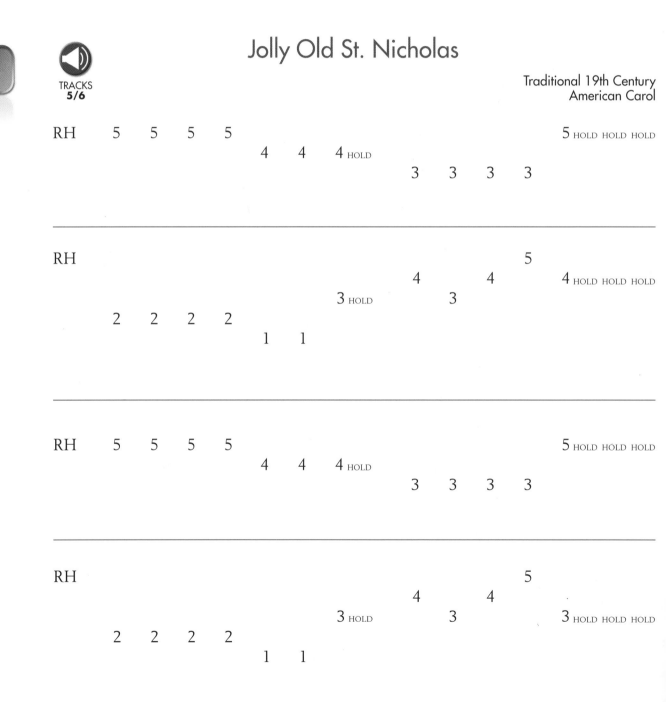

x

x

1. Place your right hand RH thumb on the lower of two black keys and your little finger on the highest of three black keys. The other fingers play the black keys in between.

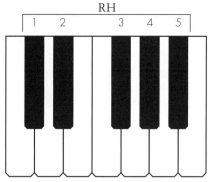

2. Say the word "hold" the number of times indicated. Remember to repeat

🔊 **TRACKS 7/8**

Matchmaker
from the Musical FIDDLER ON THE ROOF

Words by Sheldon Harnick
Music by Jerry Bock

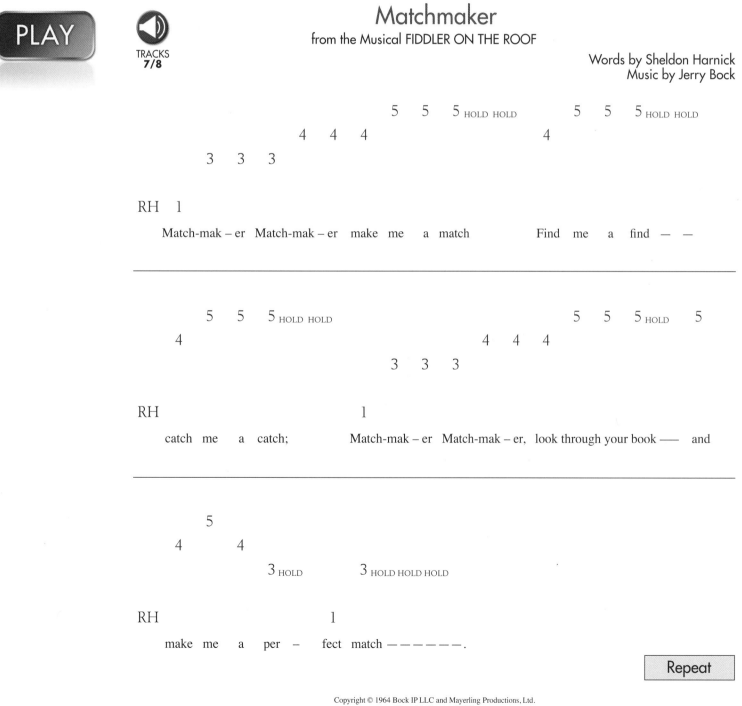

REVIEW

1. When playing piano keys on the right of the keyboard, is the sound higher or lower?

2. Which is it when playing keys on the left of the keyboard?

3. Which piano keys are in clusters, black or white?

4. Are thumbs on both hands 1 or 5?

5. Which finger number is the ring finger?

6. Which finger number is the little finger?

CHALLENGE

1. Place your LH 3rd finger on the lower of the two black keys and your RH thumb on the lowest of three black keys:

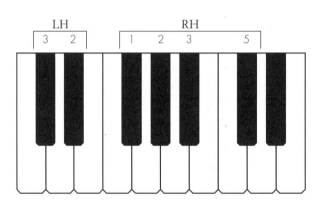

PLAY

TRACKS
9/10

Amazing Grace

Words by John Newton
Traditional American Melody

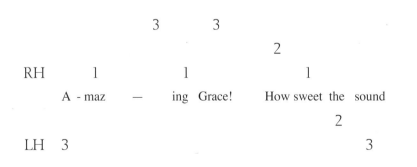

```
                                              5
                        3       3
                                      2
RH        1           1
      That  saved        a    wretch   like  me!


LH    3
```

```
              5       5
        3       3       3


RH                          1              1  1
        I   once  —   was   lost     But  now  —   am  found;
                                          2          2
LH                                        3          3
```

```
                        3       3
                                      2
RH        1           1                     1
      Was  blind        but   now     I    see.


LH    3
```

Repeat

Amazing Grace, one of the most beloved songs in the English-speaking world, was first published in 1779. John Newton, the English poet and clergyman, wrote the text for a New Year's Day sermon in 1773. For Newton, a slave trader turned abolitionist, the text was both personal and powerful in its message of conversion and redemption. The music is most currently associated with the tune *New Britain*, composed by William Walker. In its earliest form, the melody of "Amazing Grace" used only the five black keys of the piano. It was altered when it was published in a book of hymns entitled *The Southern Harmony*. *Amazing Grace* has been featured on more than 1,100 albums, and the recordings by Elvis Presley, opera singer Jessye Norman, Johnny Cash, Judy Collins, and the Royal Scots Dragoon Guards (bagpipe version) have continued to make this song an everlasting international hit.

MODULE 2
MORE KEYBOARD GEOGRAPHY

MUSIC ALPHABET

The music alphabet is the first seven letters of the English alphabet.

(A B C D E F G)

Learn it forward and backward.

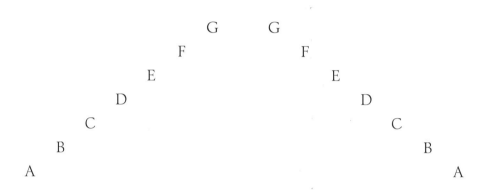

MIDDLE C

Sit in the center of the piano. A cluster of two black keys is below the piano's brand name. Middle C is the white key to the left of a cluster of these two black keys.

WHITE PIANO KEY NAMES

Learn the names of the white piano keys by their location near clusters of black keys.

C is to the left of
the two black keys

D is in the middle of
the two black keys

E is to the right of
the two black keys

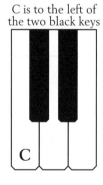

F is to the left of the
three black keys

G-A are in the middle
of the three black keys

B is to the right of
the three black keys

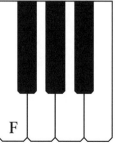

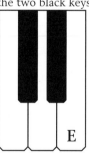

PREPARE

1. Tap or clap each square while chanting the words.

2. Play the designated alphabet letter on the correct piano key with any finger of the right or left hand. Play only on the first square of each line and chant the words.

PLAY

TRACKS
11/12

White Key Chant

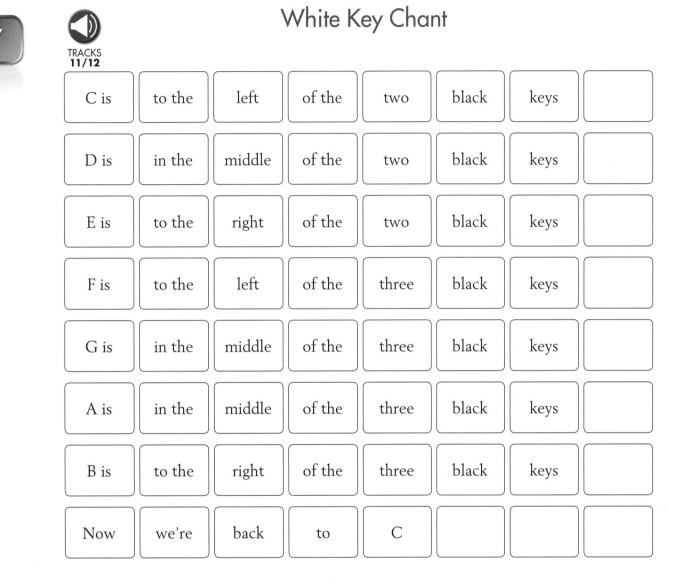

C is	to the	left	of the	two	black	keys	
D is	in the	middle	of the	two	black	keys	
E is	to the	right	of the	two	black	keys	
F is	to the	left	of the	three	black	keys	
G is	in the	middle	of the	three	black	keys	
A is	in the	middle	of the	three	black	keys	
B is	to the	right	of the	three	black	keys	
Now	we're	back	to	C			

PREPARE

1. Play the music alphabet forward and backward on the piano with your RH 2nd finger. Begin on the first A above middle C.

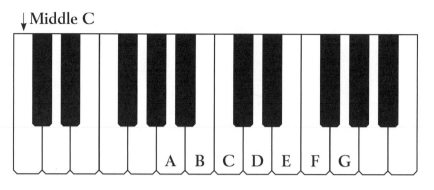

2. Play *Alphabet Waltz* by going forward in the alphabet when the notes move up and backward in the alphabet when the notes move down. Begin on the first A above middle C and play with any finger of your right or left hand.

3. White circle notes ( ) are held longer than black circle notes ( ). Count aloud while playing by saying: A HOLD B C HOLD D E HOLD (etc).

Alphabet Waltz

PLAY

TRACKS
13/14

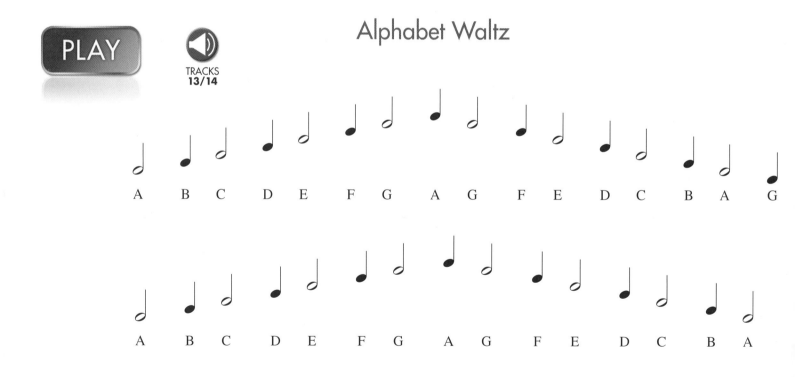

1. Place your RH 2nd finger on the second E above middle C and your LH 2nd finger on the first E above middle C.

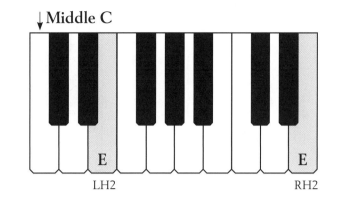

2. Play four E's (R L R L). Say the word "hold" after each.
   (E HOLD, E HOLD, E HOLD, E HOLD).
     R   L   R   L

3. The arrows below are reminders to move down one white piano key after four alphabet letters are played.

PLAY

TRACKS
15/16

Restless Theme

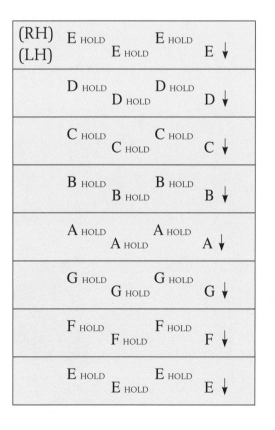

1. Place your left hand LH 5th finger on middle C and your right hand RH 5th finger on the first C above. The other fingers play the white piano keys in between without using the thumbs.

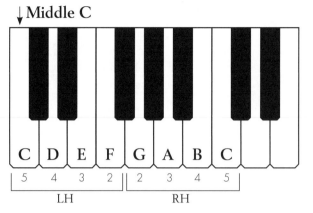

2. Sing the melody before playing it on the piano.

3. Slowly play it on the piano while observing which hand plays.

TRACKS
17/18

Joy to the World

Words by Isaac Watts
Music by George Frideric Handel

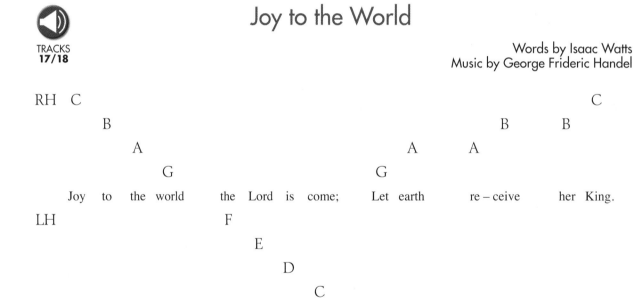

RH C C   C   C
         B   B
           A   A
             G G   G G

Let ev – ery   heart   pre – pare Him room

LH   F   F
                  E   E

RH
                    G

And heav'n and na - ture   sing, And heav'n and na - ture   sing.

LH   F   F   F
   E E   E E E   E   E
                      D   D D D

RH   C
          A
              G

And heav'n and   heav'n   and na - ture sing.

LH   F   F
   E   E   E
    D   D
    C   C

**REVIEW**

Play the requested white key and name it:

1. Play the white key to the left of the two black keys and name it.

2. Play the white key to the right of the three black keys and name it.

3. Play the white key to the right of the two black keys and name it.

4. Play the white key to the left of the three black keys and name it.

5. Play the white key in the middle of the two black keys and name it.

CHALLENGE

1. Place your RH five fingers on these piano keys (thumb on middle C).

↓ **Middle C**

| C | D | E | F | G |
| 1 | 2 | 3 | 4 | 5 |

RH

2. White circle notes ( ) are held longer than black circle notes ( ). Notes with a beam ( ) are played twice as fast as black circle notes ( ).

3. Slowly play and sing *This Land Is Your Land* before playing it with the accompaniment. Remember to say the word "hold" as many times as indicated.

This Land Is Your Land
Words and Music by Woody Guthrie
(Additional Lyrics)

V2. I've roamed and rambled and I followed my footsteps
Through the sparkling sands of her diamond deserts.
All around me, a voice was sounding,
This land was made for you and me.

V3. When the sun came shining, and I was strolling,
And the wheatfields waving, and the dust clouds rolling,
A voice was chanting, as the fog was lifting,
"This land was made for you and me."

V4. As I was walking, I saw a sign there,
And on the sign it said "No Trespassing."
But on the other side it didn't say nothing.
This side was made for you and me.

V5. In the shadow of the steeple I saw my people,
By relief office I seen my people;
As they stood there hungry, I stood there asking:
Is this land made for you and me?

V6. Nobody living can ever stop me,
As I go walking that freedom highway;
Nobody living can ever make me turn back.
This land was made for you and me.

This Land Is Your Land

Words and Music by
Woody Guthrie

MODULE 3
PRE-STAFF READING AND RHYTHM

PULSE

Music has a steady pulse. Humans have a pulse but it is not always as steady as a ticking clock or metronome. Tapping a steady pulse when listening to music is a way of "finding the beat."

RHYTHM

Music has different kinds of notes called rhythms. The way they are formed determines the number of pulses they are held.

♩	Quarter note	Black circle with stem	One pulse
♩	Half note	White circle with stem	Two pulses
♩.	Dotted half note	White circle with dot and stem	Three pulses
o	Whole note	White circle, no stem	Four pulses

COUNTING RHYTHMS

There is not a right or wrong way to count, but it is helpful to be consistent. One way is to talk the kind of rhythm. Think of each box below as a pulse.

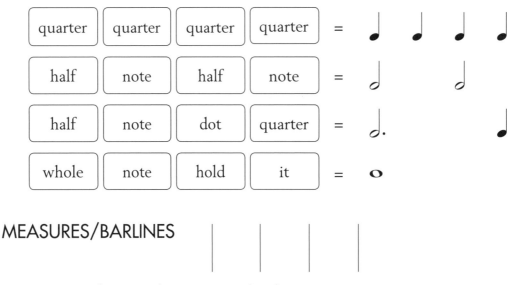

MEASURES/BARLINES

A measure is the space between two bar lines.

TIE

When repeated notes are connected by a curved line, the second note is held and not played.

PREPARE

1. An easy way to start reading music is to see it separated from the lines and spaces which is pre-staff reading. Begin with the 3rd finger of the RH on E above middle C and play *Ode to Joy* with finger numbers.

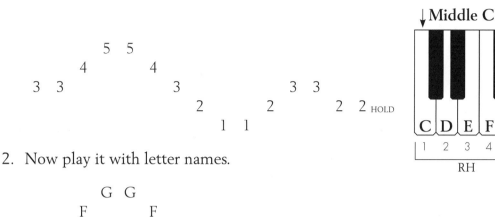

2. Now play it with letter names.

3. After hearing the introduction on track 21, play the top line below with the RH before playing the bottom line with the LH. The LH begins with the 3rd finger on the first E below middle C. Hold the quarter notes one pulse and the half notes two pulses.

PLAY

TRACKS
21/22

Ode to Joy
from SYMPHONY NO. 9 IN D MINOR

Ludwig van Beethoven

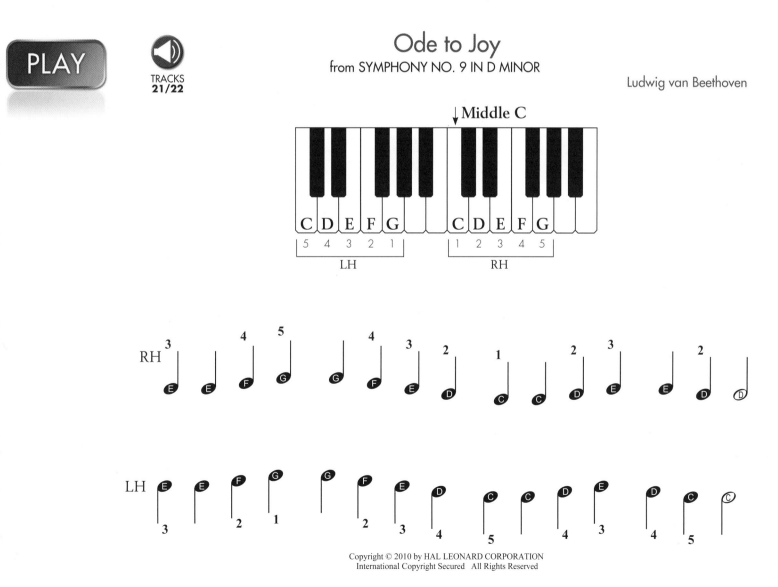

1. Place your RH five fingers on these piano keys (thumb on middle C). Slowly play and talk the finger numbers in *Beautiful Brown Eyes*. Quarter notes are one pulse, half notes are two pulses, and dotted half notes are three pulses. Remember to hold the tied note (do not play it again).

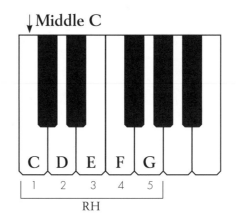

2. Now place your LH five fingers on these piano keys (little finger on C below middle C). Slowly play and talk the letter names in *Beautiful Brown Eyes*. Begin with the 3rd finger of the LH.

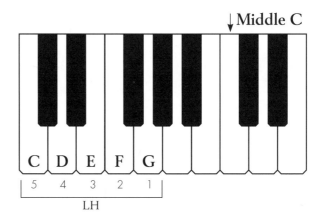

3. Have both hands on correct piano keys before playing with accompaniment.

Beautiful Brown Eyes

Traditional

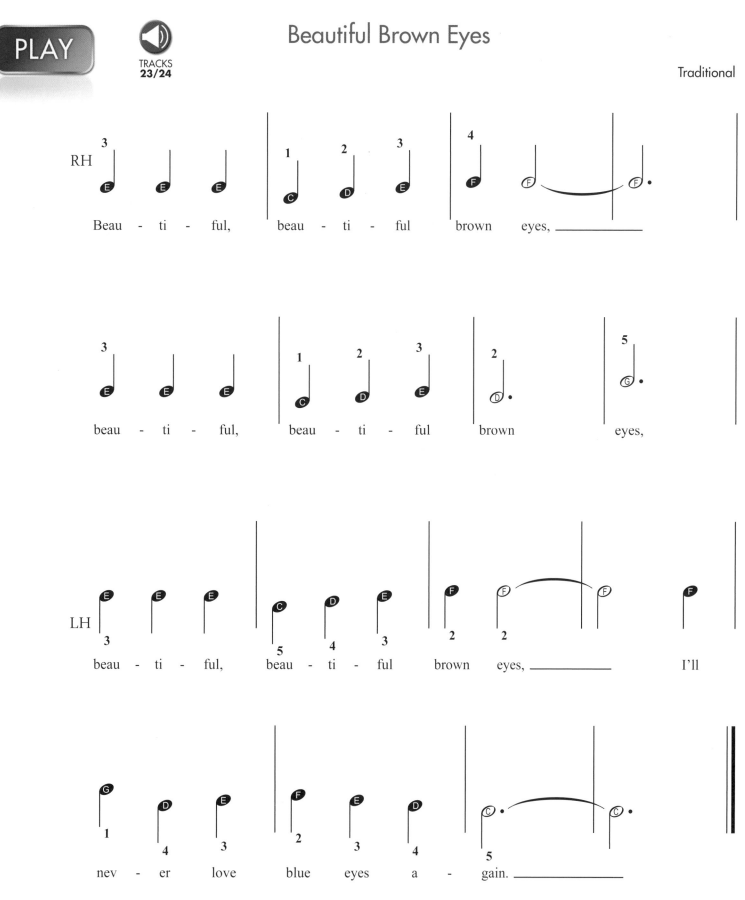

1. Place your RH fingers on C D E F G and slowly play and talk the finger numbers in *Aura Lee*. Next place your LH fingers on C D E F G and slowly play and talk the LH finger numbers.

2. Remember to repeat.

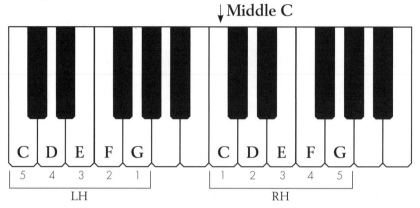

PLAY

TRACKS
25/26

Aura Lee

Words by W.W. Fosdick
Music by George R. Poulton

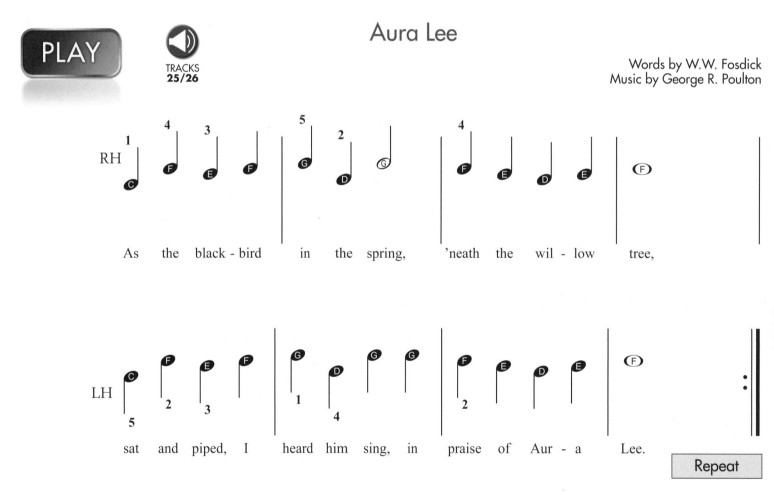

Repeat

PREPARE

1. Place your RH five fingers on the 5 piano keys with the thumb on middle C. Place your LH five fingers on the 5 piano keys with the thumb on F below middle C. Alternate the hands as indicated.

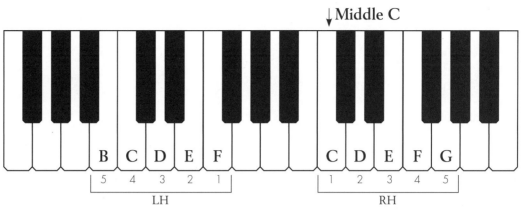

2. Slowly play and talk the finger numbers in *Marianne*. Quarter notes are one pulse, half notes are two pulses and whole notes are four pulses. Remember to hold the tied note (do not play it again).

PLAY

TRACKS
27/28

Marianne

Traditional

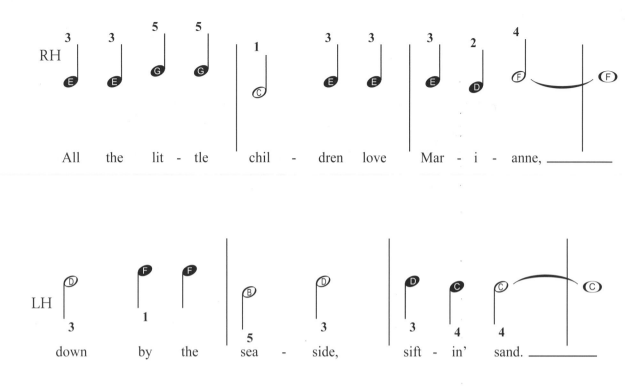

All the lit - tle chil - dren love Mar - i - anne, _____

down by the sea - side, sift - in' sand. _____

1. Which rhythm in this module is held the longest and what is it called?

2. Which note is held the shortest and what is it called?

3. Which rhythm has no stem?

4. Which rhythm has a stem, a white circle and a dot?

5. Name the kind of note that is held 4 pulses.

6. Name the kind of note that is held 2 pulses.

7. Name the kind of note that is held 3 pulses.

8. Name the kind of note that is held 1 pulse.

9. How many pulses are in a measure that has a quarter note and a half note?

10. How many pulses are in a measure that has two half notes?

11. How many pulses are in a measure that has a dotted half note and a quarter note?

12. How many pulses are in a measure that has a whole note?

13. How many pulses are in a measure that has a half note tied to a half note?

14. What is the name for a curved line connecting a repeated note?

15. Name an object that has a steady pulse.

CHALLENGE

1. Place your RH and LH fingers on these piano keys. The LH thumb is on middle C and the RH thumb is on the D above middle C.

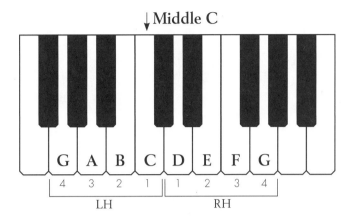

2. Slowly play and talk the finger numbers of *Can You Feel the Love Tonight*. Quarter notes are one pulse, half notes are two pulses, dotted half notes are three pulses and whole notes are four pulses. Remember to hold the tied notes and not play them again.

3. Repeat signs and first and second endings are used when a section of a song is repeated.

𝄆   𝄇 – Play the section between the double bars twice.

┌───────┬────────┐
│1.   │2.   │ – After playing first ending, repeat the designated section
                    and jump to the second ending.

Can You Feel the Love Tonight
from Walt Disney Pictures' THE LION KING

Music by Elton John
Lyrics by Tim Rice

PLAY

TRACKS
29/30

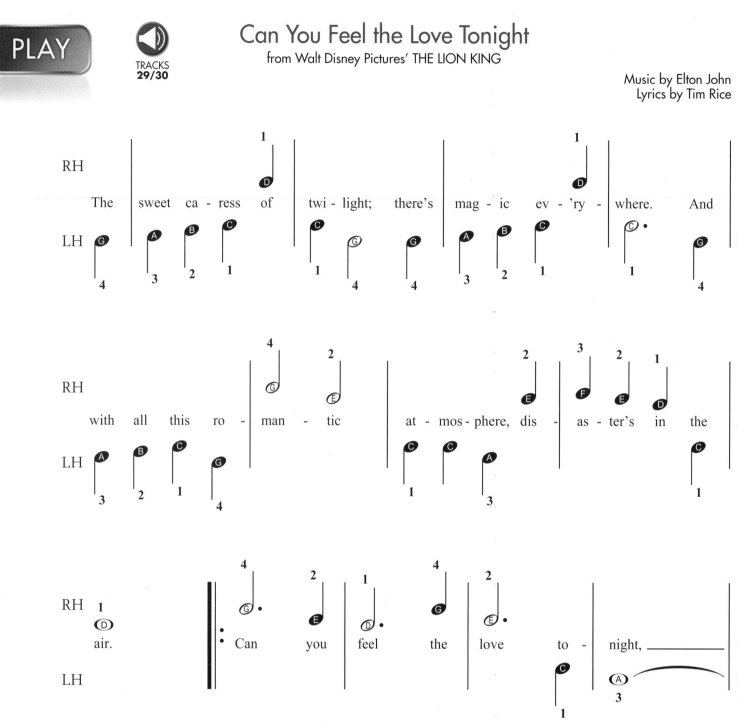

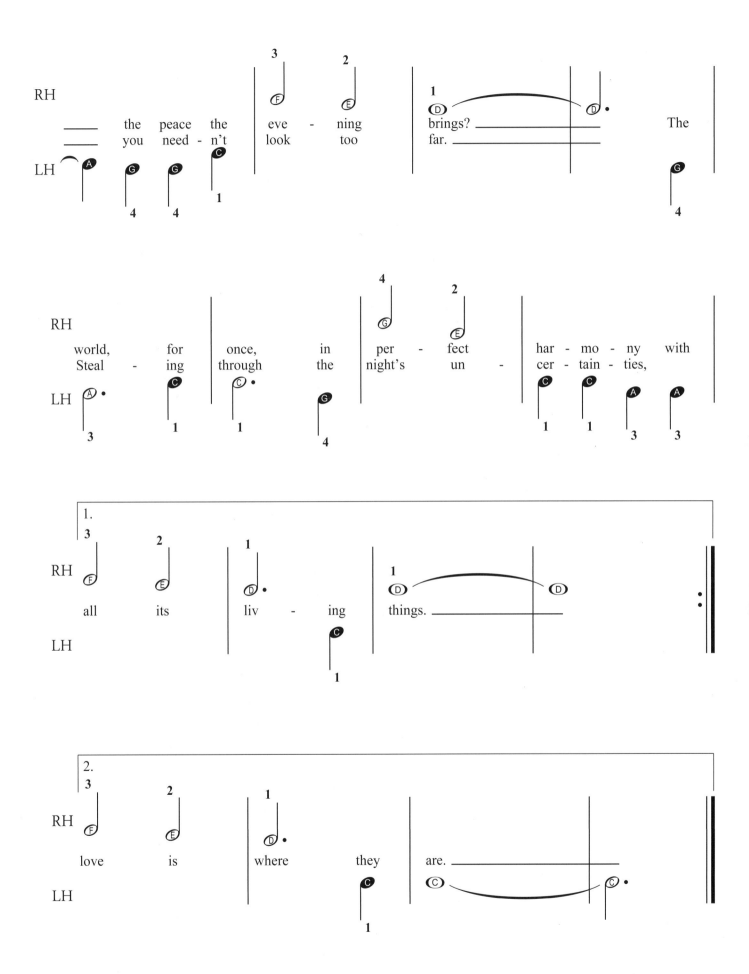

MODULE 4
GRAND STAFF

GRAND STAFF COMPONENTS

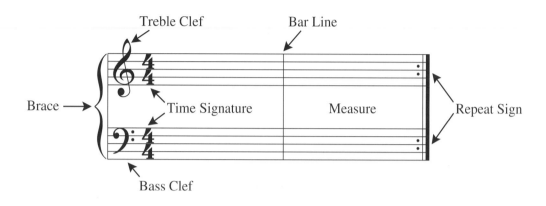

NAMES OF LINES AND SPACES ON BOTH CLEFS
Treble clef notes are usually played by the RH.

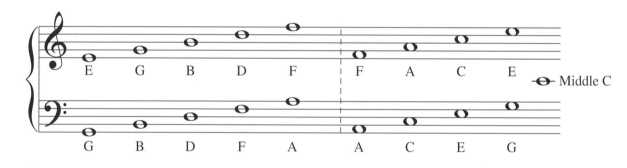

Bass clef notes are usually played by the LH.

TIPS FOR QUICK LEARNING
Four of the lines on both clefs have the same alphabet letters (G B D F). To learn the treble, say E and quickly name G B D F.

To learn bass, quickly say G B D F, followed by A.

Three of the spaces on both clefs spell the word A C E. To learn the treble, say F followed by A C E.

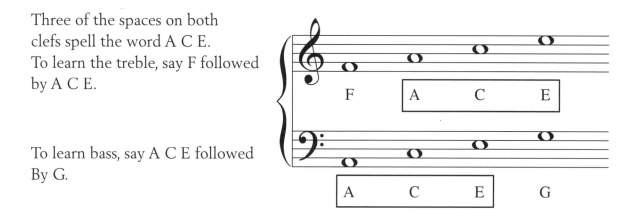

To learn bass, say A C E followed By G.

FINDING GRAND STAFF NOTES ON THE KEYBOARD

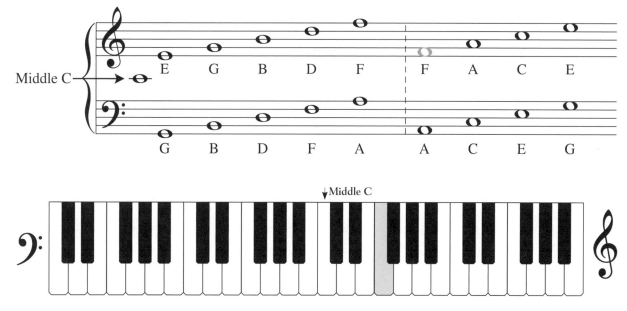

The treble clef notes above are to the right of middle C and the bass clef notes are to the left. Find all the grand staff notes on the keyboard and describe where they are in relation to middle C. For example, 1st space F in the treble clef in the example above is the first F to the right of middle C.

TIME SIGNATURES

Music is sound organized in time. Musicians organize pulses or beats into measures. A time signature is one number above another. It is not written as a fraction (4/4). The top number tells the number of pulses per measure and the bottom number tells the pulse note.

4 = 4 pulses per measure

4 = is pulse note

1. Reading music is easier when the lines and spaces on both clefs are memorized. Chants reinforce memory. After hearing the introduction on track 31, say the words to *Treble Clef Chant*. Do not write in the names of the lines and spaces. Memorize, memorize, memorize! Repeat measures 1 – 4 and measures 15 – 18.

Treble Clef Chant

TRACK
31

Treble clef 5 lines, name those notes: ___ ___ ___ ___ ___ hold, hold, hold.

5
What's on the **1st** line? Name that note ___ What's on the **3rd** line? Name that note ___

9
What's on the **5th** line? Name that note ___ What's on the **4th** line? Name that note ___

13
What's on the **2nd** line? Name that note ___ Treble clef 4 spaces name those notes:

17
___ ___ ___ ___ What's on the **1st** space? Name that note ___

21
What's on the **3rd** space? Name that note ___ What's on the **2nd** space? Name that note ___

25
What's on the **4th** space? Name that note ___ Learn this chant so you'll know your notes!

1. After hearing the introduction on track 32, say the words to *Bass Clef Chant*. Do not write the names of the lines and spaces. Memorize, memorize, memorize! Repeat measures 1 – 4 and measures 15 – 18.

TRACK
32

Bass Clef Chant 𝄢:

Bass clef 5 lines, name those notes: ___ ___ ___ ___ ___ hold, hold, hold.

What's on the **5th** line? Name that note ___ What's on the **1st** line? Name that note ___

What's on the **2nd** line? Name that note ___ What's on the **3rd** line? Name that note ___

What's on the **4th** line? Name that note ___ Bass clef 4 spaces name those notes:

___ ___ ___ ___ What's on the **4th** space? Name that note ___

What's on the **1st** space? Name that note ___ What's on the **2nd** space? Name that note ___

What's on the **3rd** space? Name that note ___ Learn this chant so you'll know your notes!

Answer these questions while looking at the corresponding shaded numbers on *Que Sera, Sera* on page 37.

1. Name the clef sign used?

2. Explain the two numbers of the time signature. How many pulses per measure and what is the pulse note?

3. What is the name of the first note and why does it have that special name?

4. This note was not identified in the lines and spaces chant on p. 32. Since it is between C and E, what is its name?

5. Name the notes for "I asked my mother" without writing them.

6. How many pulses is the tied F-note held?

7. Name the notes for "Will I be rich?" without writing them.

8. What is this note's name since it comes before Middle C?

9. How many pulses should each measure have in $\frac{3}{4}$ time? Since there are two quarter notes getting one pulse each, how might you explain the 𝄽 on the 1st beat of this measure? (Hint: See first page of Module 6.)

10. What is the name of this note and how many pulses is it held?

11. Name the notes for "Whatever will be, will be" without writing them. Are there more line notes or space notes?

12. Are there more line or space notes on "The future's not ours to see."

13. How many pulses is the last note held? What is its letter name?

14. If you know *Que Sera, Sera*, sing the words with the accompaniment.

Que Sera, Sera
(Whatever Will Be, Will Be)

Words and Music by
Jay Livingston and Ray Evans

MODULE 5
DIRECTIONAL READING

DIRECTIONAL READING

In beginning piano music, notes usually move in three directions: repeat, step up or down, and skip up or down.

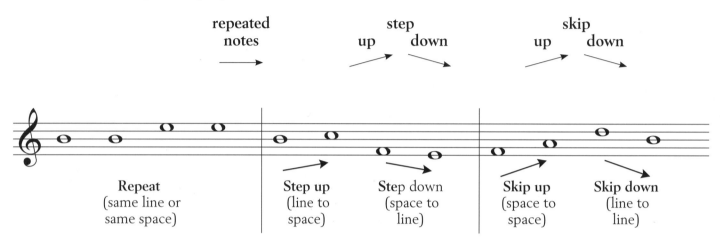

To read music on the staff directionally, name the beginning note and play it with the finger number above the note. You learned *Beautiful Brown Eyes* off staff on p. 25. It began on the first E above middle C. Slowly play *Beautiful Brown Eyes* as you say each direction (as written below).

Beautiful Brown Eyes

Traditional

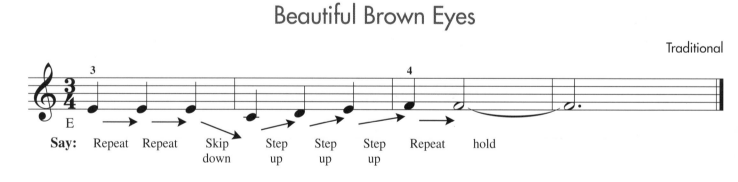

Follow this process to learn music on the staff:

1. Clap and say the rhythm.

2. Say or sing the finger numbers and play them in the air.

3. Say or sing the names of notes and play them in the air.

4. Play right and left hand separately on the piano while saying each direction (steps and repeats).

5. Play the piece slowly while talking the rhythm. (i.e., quar-ter, quar-ter, quar-ter, etc.)

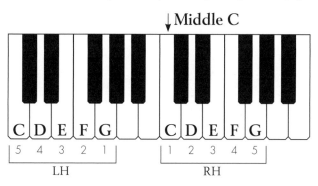

PLAY TRACKS **21/22**

Ode to Joy
from SYMPHONY NO. 9 IN D MINOR

Ludwig van Beethoven

TRACKS
23/24

Beautiful Brown Eyes

Traditional

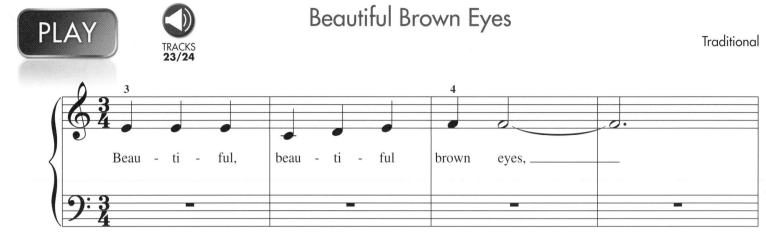

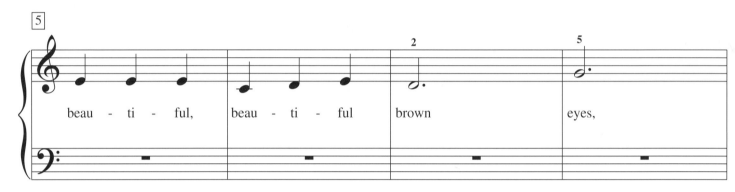

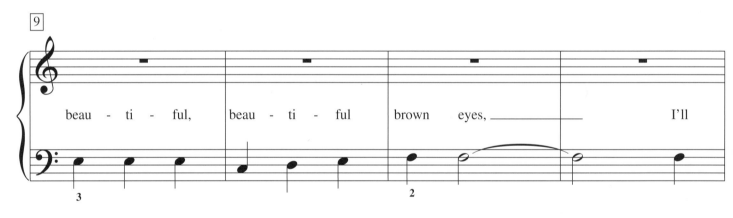

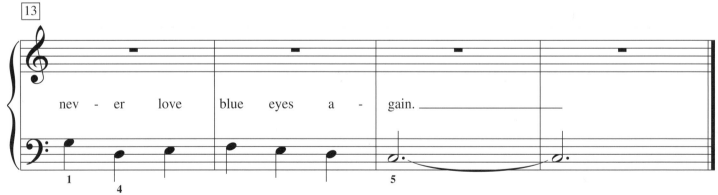

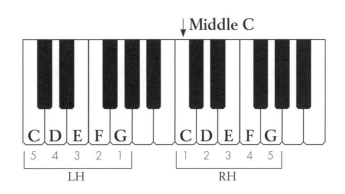

Middle C

Skips can skip more than one piano key and alphabet letter. (C D E F)

Aura Lee

TRACKS
25/26

Words by W.W. Foskick
Music by George R. Poulton

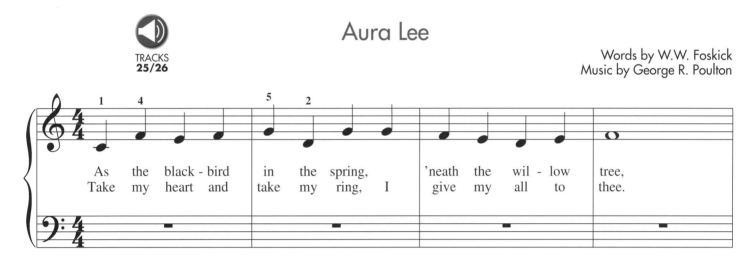

As the black-bird in the spring, 'neath the wil - low tree,
Take my heart and take my ring, I give my all to thee.

sat and piped, I heard him sing, in praise of Au - ra Lee.
Take me for e - ter - ni - ty, dear - est Au - ra Lee.

Preparation for *I Walk the Line*.

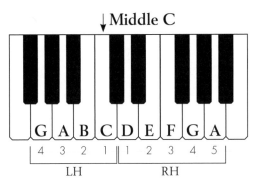

1. Place your RH five fingers with the thumb on D above middle C. Place your LH four fingers with your thumb on middle C. Your two thumbs are next to each other.

2. Slowly play and say the rhythm. Quarter notes are one pulse, half notes are two pulses and whole notes are four pulses. Remember to hold the tied notes and do not play them again.

3. Slowly play and say the finger numbers.

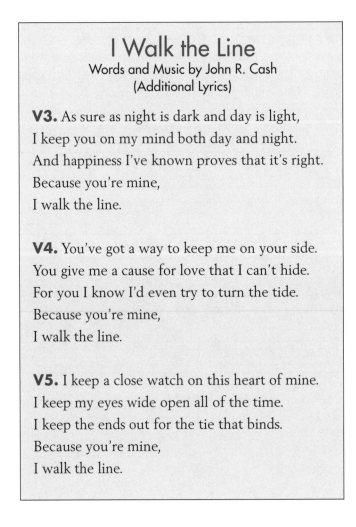

I Walk the Line
Words and Music by John R. Cash
(Additional Lyrics)

V3. As sure as night is dark and day is light,
I keep you on my mind both day and night.
And happiness I've known proves that it's right.
Because you're mine,
I walk the line.

V4. You've got a way to keep me on your side.
You give me a cause for love that I can't hide.
For you I know I'd even try to turn the tide.
Because you're mine,
I walk the line.

V5. I keep a close watch on this heart of mine.
I keep my eyes wide open all of the time.
I keep the ends out for the tie that binds.
Because you're mine,
I walk the line.

I Walk the Line

Words and Music by
John R. Cash

PLAY

TRACKS
34/35

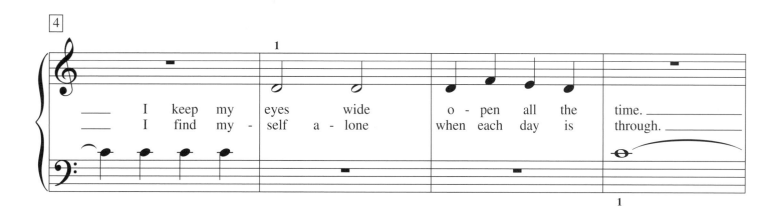

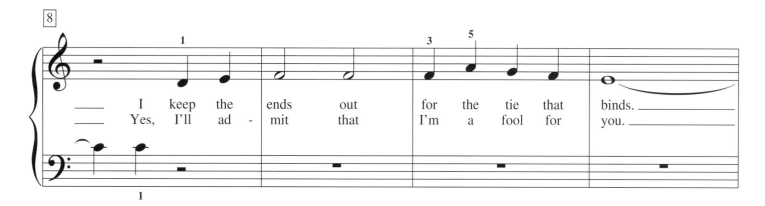

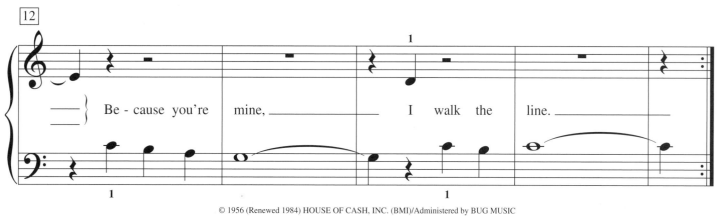

HANDS TOGETHER

1. Playing a piece hands together is a challenge at first. It is best mastered by first learning hands separately. Slowly analyze each beat with hands together by saying it aloud and patting your knees. In the first measure of *Ode to Joy* below, the beats are:

Beat 1	Beat 2	Beat 3	Beat 4
Together	Right	Together	Right
(Pat both knees)	(Pat right knee)	(Pat both knees)	(Pat right knee)

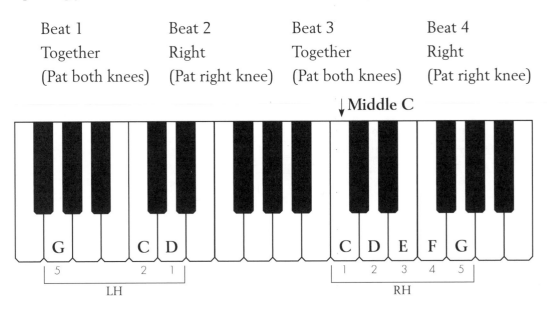

2. To learn the LH separately, place your LH thumb on D below middle C and the other fingers are on the white keys below the D. Learn the LH by playing this pattern as half notes, holding each one for two beats:

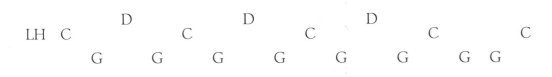

Ode to Joy
from SYMPHONY NO. 9 IN D MINOR

Ludwig van Beethoven

MODULE 6
MORE RHYTHM

EIGHTH NOTES

Eighth notes create more movement in music as they are shorter in duration. Two eighth notes equal one quarter note and both eighth notes must be played on one pulse.

8th   8th   quar-ter

A single eighth note by itself has a flag. (♪) Two eighths together are connected by a beam. (♫)

DOTTED QUARTER NOTES

A dot after a note lengthens the time the note is held by half the value of the note. A dotted quarter note is equal to a quarter note tied to an eighth note:

1 pulse   ½ pulse   1½ pulses (or beats)

Dotted quarter notes are often followed by an eighth note so they are counted:

quar - ter   dot   8th

RESTS

A rest is a silence. Notes symbolize sounds and rests symbolize silence.

Quarter Rest	**Half Rest**	**Whole Rest**
1 pulse of silence	Sits on 3rd line 2 pulses of silence	Hangs from 4th line 4 pulses of silence

COUNTING ALOUD WITH EIGHTH NOTES

1. Before playing *Hush Little Baby* on the piano, slowly clap and speak the rhythm several times. Next clap and speak the rhythm while listening to the audio.

2. The first beat of every other measure begins with a G in the left hand and a quarter rest in the right hand.

PLAY

TRACKS
36/37

Hush, Little Baby

Carolina Folk Melody

COUNTING ALOUD WITH DOTTED QUARTER AND EIGHTH NOTES

1. Before playing *Alouette* on the piano, slowly clap and speak the rhythm several times.

2. Next, slowly clap and speak the rhythm while listening to the audio.

Alouette

French Folk Song

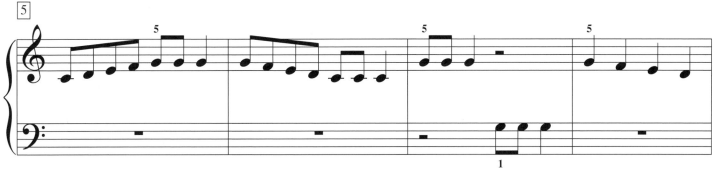

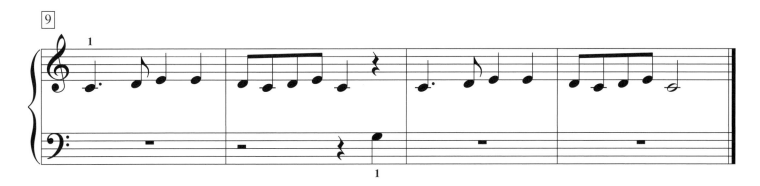

PREPARE

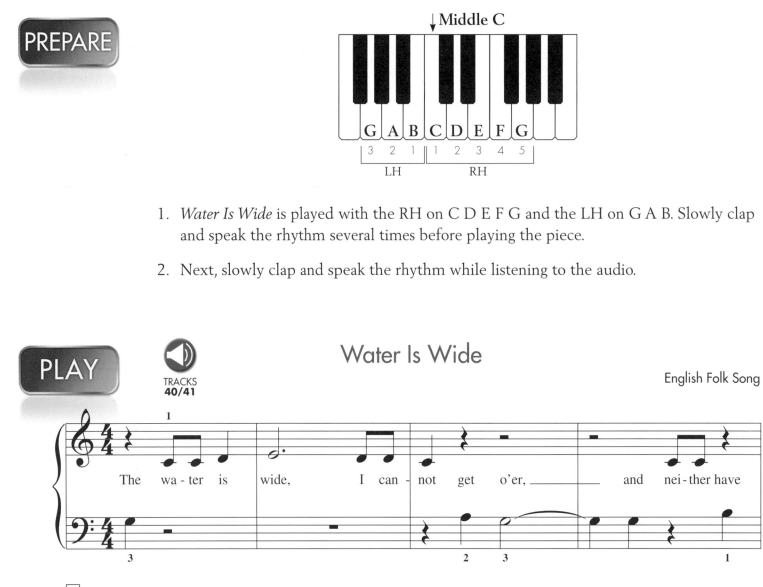

1. *Water Is Wide* is played with the RH on C D E F G and the LH on G A B. Slowly clap and speak the rhythm several times before playing the piece.

2. Next, slowly clap and speak the rhythm while listening to the audio.

PLAY

TRACKS
40/41

Water Is Wide

English Folk Song

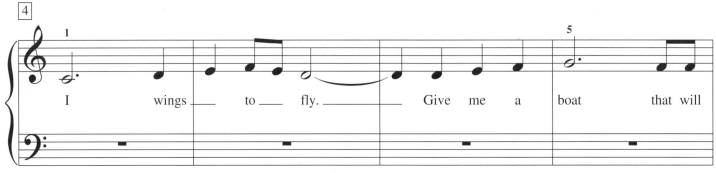

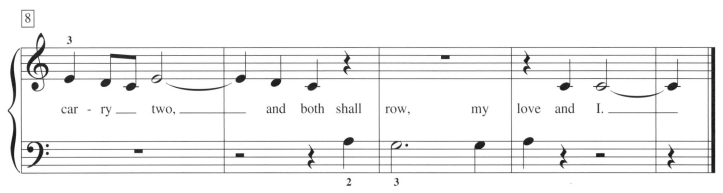

1. Place your RH five fingers on the 5 piano keys with the thumb on F above middle C. Place your LH five fingers on the 5 piano keys with the thumb on E above middle C.

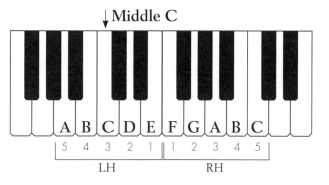

2. In *Don't Be Cruel* (p. 50) and *Danny Boy* (p. 52) there are some new LH notes. Beginning with the top line A on the bass clef, they are the first five letters of the alphabet.

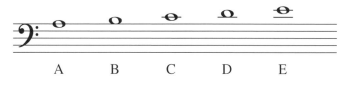

3. Spell these words under these notes.

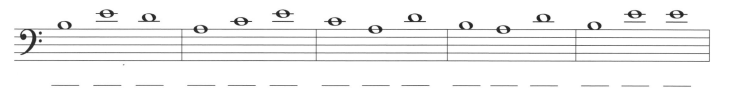

4. Slowly clap and speak the rhythm of *Don't Be Cruel*. Remember to hold the tied notes over the barline and do not restrike.

5. Slowly play and speak the finger numbers while playing *Don't Be Cruel* with the accompaniment.

Don't Be Cruel
(To a Heart That's True)

Words and Music by Otis Blackwell
and Elvis Presley

You know I can be found
Ba - by, if I made you

sit - ting home all a - lone. If
some-thing I might have said,

you can't come a -
please let's for - get the

round, at least, please tel - e -
past; at the fu - ture looks bright a -

phone.} Don't be
head.

cruel _____ to a heart that's true. _____

REVIEW

1. What kind of note is half the value of a quarter note?

2. If an eighth note by itself has a flag, what connects two eighth notes?

3. What kind of rest looks like a bird flying sideways?

4. What kind of rest hangs from the 4th line?

5. What kind of rest sits on the 3rd line?

6. If notes symbolize sounds, what do rests symbolize?

1. *Danny Boy* is played with two different hand positions. Place both hands on Position 1 and slowly play the first 16 measures of *Danny Boy*. Place both hands on Position 2 and slowly play the next 8 measures. Play the last 8 measures on Position 1.

2. Review the 5 bass clef notes on page 49 by saying the note names while playing them.

3. Slowly clap and talk the rhythm of *Danny Boy*. Remember to hold the tied note.

4. Slowly play and talk the finger numbers of *Danny Boy*. The challenge will be quickly moving back and forth between the two hand positions.

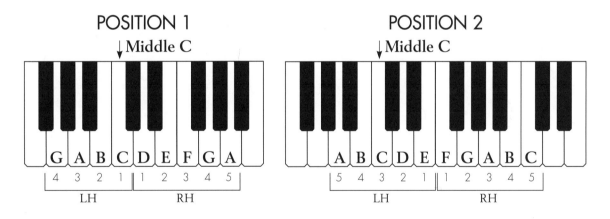

Danny Boy

Words by Frederick Edward Weatherly
Traditional Irish Folk Melody

Position 1

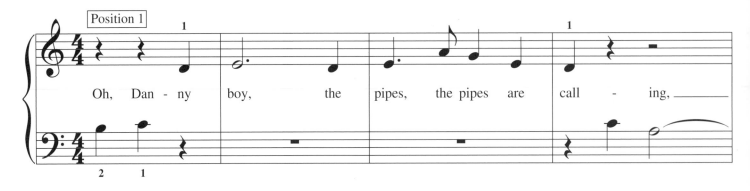

Oh, Dan-ny boy, the pipes, the pipes are call-ing,

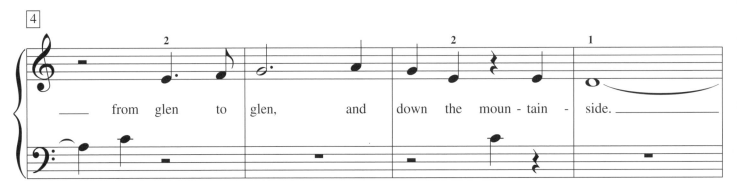

___ from glen to glen, and down the moun-tain-side. ___

___ The sum-mer's gone, and all the ros-es fall-ing,

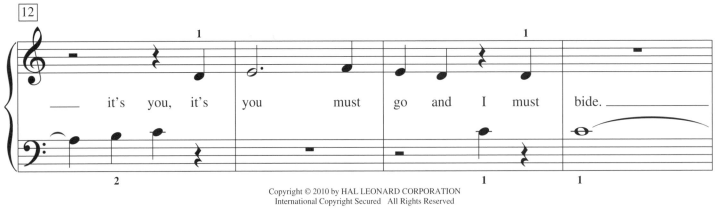

___ it's you, it's you must go and I must bide. ___

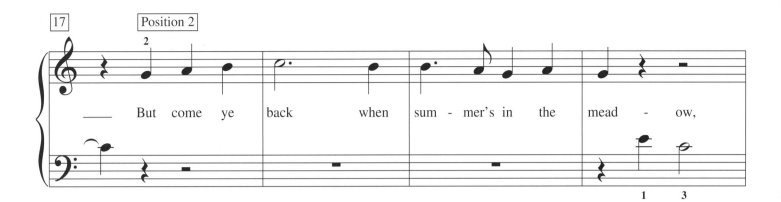

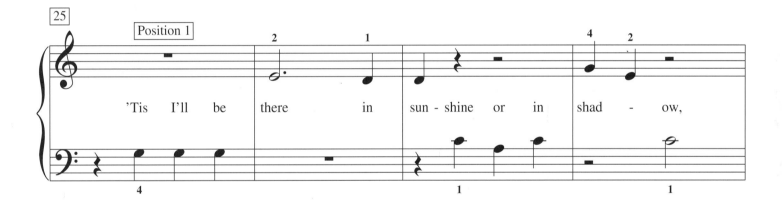

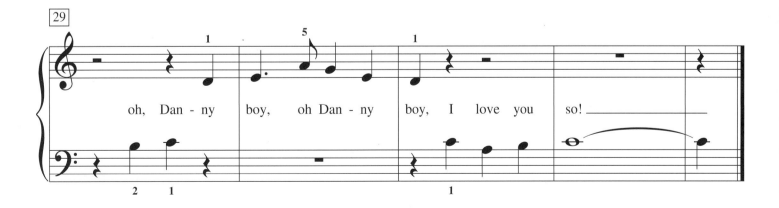

MODULE 7
CHORDS AND LEAD SHEETS

TRIADS – ROOT POSITION

A triad is a three-note chord. It can be built on any piano key. The bottom note is the root, the middle note is the 3rd and the top note is the 5th. When it is built on the root, the note names skip every other letter of the alphabet. The RH fingering is usually 1-3-5 and the LH fingering is usually 5-3-1.

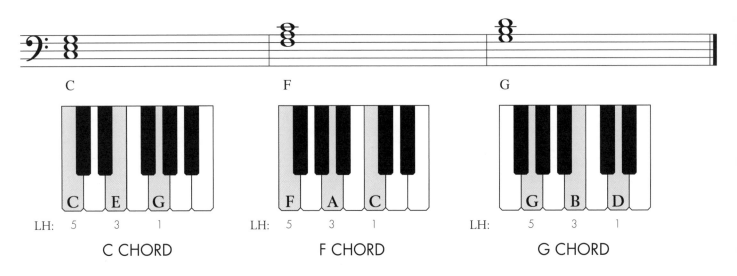

SEVENTH CHORDS

A seventh (7th) chord has four notes. The bottom note is the root, the next note above is the 3rd, the note above the 3rd is the 5th, and the top note is the 7th.

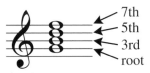

LEAD SHEETS

A lead sheet is a RH melody with alphabet letters (chord symbols) written above the melody. Piano music usually has notes written in both clefs. It will often, however, have alphabet letters above the melody to indicate chords that could harmonize the melody.

PLAYING LEAD SHEETS

When the Saints Go Marching In is an example of a lead sheet. The alphabet letter above each measure indicates the LH triad to be played. These triads sound best when they are played in the range just below middle C.

1. Learn the LH chords first before playing hands together.

2. Next, hum the melody while playing the LH chords.

3. Slowly play the chords and the melody together. Move the RH melody to the first C above middle C so the hands do not get in each other's way.

PLAY

TRACKS
46/47

When the Saints Go Marching In

Words by Katherine E. Purvis
Music by James M. Black

CLOSE POSITION

Remember that chords sound best when they are played in the range below middle C. They are also easier to play in close position rather than root position. Close position is found by moving to the nearest chord tones rather than having the hand move from root to root.

The chords for *I Know Where I'm Goin'* are:

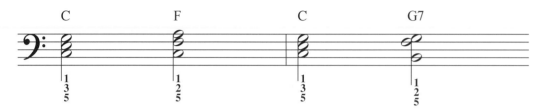

The G7 chord has four notes (G B D F), but the 5th (D) is sometimes omitted. This simplified G7 chord has only three notes (B F G).

1. Before adding the RH melody, learn the LH chords in close position by practicing the finger movements from chord to chord.

2. Next, hum the melody while playing the LH chords.

3. Slowly play the chords and the melody together.

I Know Where I'm Goin'

English Folksong

TRACKS
48/49

1. Practice the LH triads in close position.
   • The alphabet letter above each measure indicates the LH triad to be played.
   • Triads sound best when they are played in the range just below middle C.

2. Next play the LH triads and hum the melody.

3. Slowly play the triads and melody together.

4. The 2nd finger is circled on measure 8 since it replaces finger 3 on G.

TRACKS
50/51

Oh, Lonesome Me

Words and Music by
Don Gibson

REVIEW

1. Spell and play the C triad.

2. Spell and play the F triad.

3. Spell and play the G triad.

4. Spell and play the G7 chord (all 4 letter names).

5. If a triad is built on the root, what are the chord numbers of the top two notes?

6. In a 7th chord, which chord number is sometimes omitted, the 5th or the 7th?

7. What color are the piano keys for the C, F and G triads?

8. What are three-note chords called?

9. In a lead sheet, where do we find the chord symbols?

10. Why do we play LH chords in the range just below middle C?

CHALLENGE

1. Practice the LH C, F and G7 close position chords until the hand moves effortlessly from chord to chord.

2. In *My Heart Will Go On*, slowly clap and speak the rhythm of the RH melody.

3. Practice the RH melody alone paying close attention to the finger numbers. The circled finger number in measure 12 indicates that the 4th finger should play the E. In measure 15, the 2nd finger is circled because it crosses over the thumb.

4. Practice the LH as written and hum the melody to *My Heart Will Go On*.

5. Slowly play the chords and the melody together.

My Heart Will Go On
(Love Theme from 'Titanic')
from the Paramount and Twentieth Century Fox Motion Picture TITANIC

Music by James Horner
Lyrics by Will Jennings

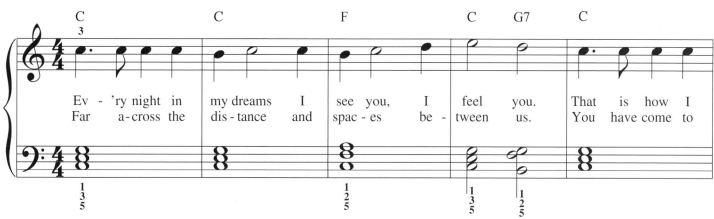

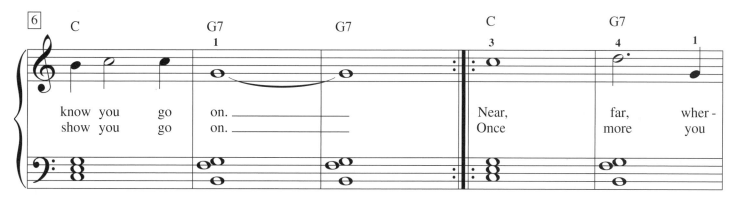

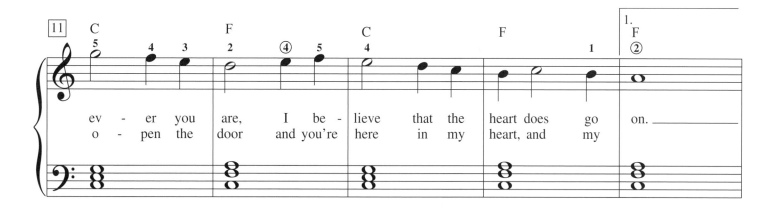

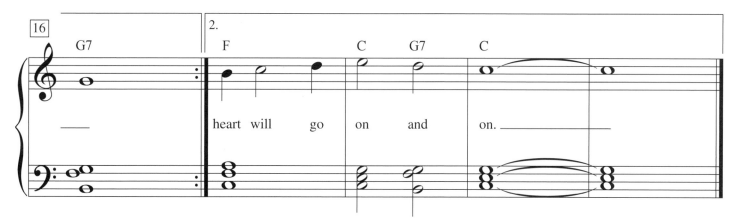

MODULE 8
MAJOR AND MINOR TRIADS

MAJOR TRIADS

The easiest way to learn triads (3-note chords) is by their shape. The shape for the F major triad is ▢▢▢. It is every other white piano key, every other space on the treble clef, and it is played with every other finger. (RH= 1 3 5 and LH= 5 3 1)

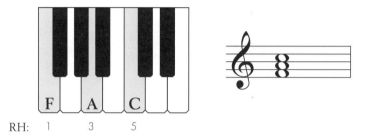

The shape for the D major triad is ▢■▢. Since the middle note is a black key, finger 3 plays F♯ (sharp) instead of F♮ (natural). To sharp a note, play the next piano key to the right which may be white or black.

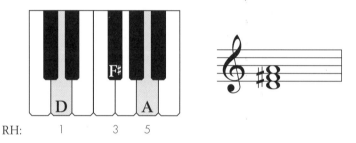

THREE SETS OF MAJOR TRIADS

Triads built on white piano keys of the piano may be divided into three patterns or sets:

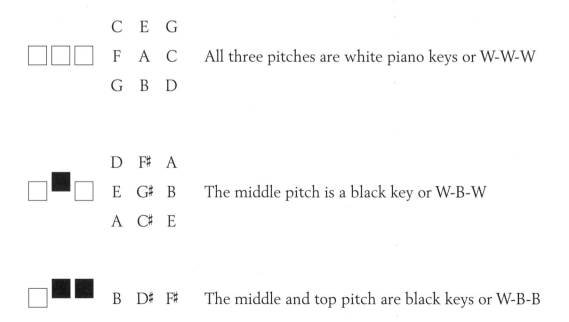

▢▢▢	C E G F A C G B D	All three pitches are white piano keys or W-W-W
▢■▢	D F♯ A E G♯ B A C♯ E	The middle pitch is a black key or W-B-W
▢■■	B D♯ F♯	The middle and top pitch are black keys or W-B-B

CHANGE MAJOR TRIADS TO MINOR

A minor triad is created by lowering the middle note of a major triad to the very next piano key (which may be black or white).

- A flat (♭) lowers a white-key note to a black-key note.

- A natural (♮) lowers a black-key note (♯) to a white-key note.

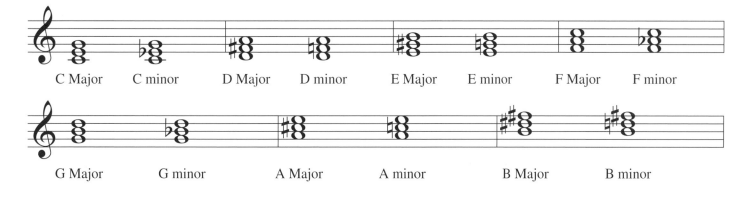

1. In *Scarborough Fair,* only the roots for each LH triad are shown. Add the missing 3rd and 5th to each triad to create the LH accompaniment. Slowly play the LH triads alone. A plain alphabet letter indicates major (C = C E G) and a small "m" by a letter indicates minor (Dm = D F A).

2. Practice the RH melody with the finger numbers that are marked. In measure 12, finger 3 is circled because it crosses over the thumb. In measure 15, finger 2 is circled because it crosses over the thumb.

3. Slowly play the melody with LH triads before playing with the audio.

PLAY

TRACKS
54/55

Scarborough Fair

Traditional English

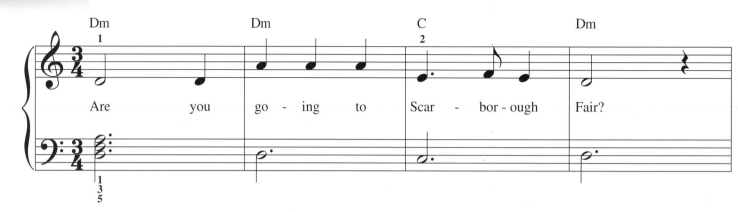

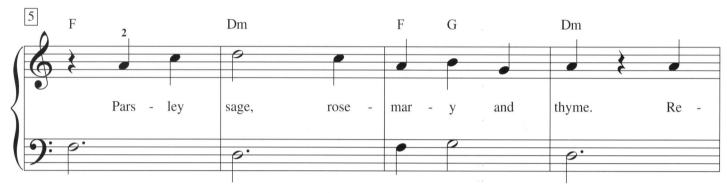

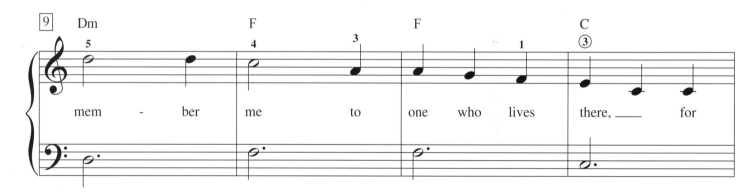

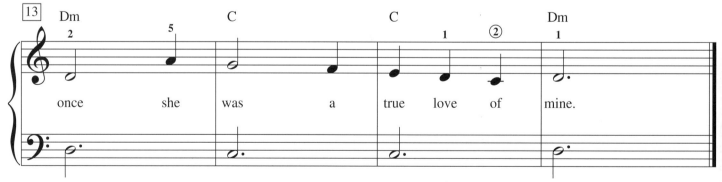

1. Spell the LH triads found in *Unchained Melody* on p. 64. The small m indicates minor.

   G = _____   _____   _____

   Em = _____   _____   _____

   C = _____   _____   _____

   D = _____   _____   _____

   Bm = _____   _____   _____

2. Play the LH triads in the octave below middle C (root or close position).

3. Play the RH of *Unchained Melody* an octave higher than written with the finger numbers that are marked. Finger 3 is circled in measure 9 to indicate a hand shift from measures 7-8. The thumb is circled in measure 14 to indicate a hand shift (thumb on G).

4. Measures 4, 12 and 20 have a sharp sign in front of the F. To sharp a note, play the next piano key to the right (F♯ instead of F♮).

5. Slowly play the melody with the LH triads. The pattern for the first 12 measures is:

G	Em	C	D
G	Em	D	D
G	Em	C	D

Unchained Melody
from the Motion Picture UNCHAINED

Lyrics by Hy Zaret
Music by Alex North

REVIEW

1. Which three major triads are white-black-white?

2. Which three major triads are white-white-white?

3. Which major triad is white-black-black?

4. How does a major triad become a minor triad?

5. If the middle note of a major triad is a white key, what color does it become when it's changed to minor?

6. If the middle note of a major triad is a black key, what color does it become when it's changed to minor?

CHALLENGE

1. Spell the LH triads found in *Try to Remember* on p. 66. The small m indicates minor.

G   =   ____   ____   ____

Em   =   ____   ____   ____

Am   =   ____   ____   ____

D   =   ____   ____   ____

Bm   =   ____   ____   ____

C   =   ____   ____   ____

2. Play the LH triads in the octave below middle C (root or close position).

3. Play the RH melody an octave higher than written with the finger numbers that are marked. Play the F♯ in measure 24.

4. The pattern for measures 1-16 and 25 to the end is:

G   Em   Am   D

5. Slowly play the melody with the LH triads.

Try to Remember
from THE FANTASTICKS

Words by Tom Jones
Music by Harvey Schmidt

APPENDIX
10 FAQs about RMM Teaching

1. **Can Piano Fun for Adult Beginners be taught to an individual student as well as to a class?**

   Yes it can. However, it has proven to be especially successful with groups. The class tends to bond and become a support group for each other. As long as solo playing is voluntary, class members are not hesitant about coming to class even if their practice time has been minimal that week.

2. **How do I group my students?**

   Many RMM programs start with a beginner class. If the program has multiple levels of classes, I invite new students to visit different levels and together we determine which class is best for their skill level. Usually the students wait for the next enrollment period to join the appropriate group.

3. **Will every student in a class be at the same skill level?**

   Even if they begin that way, they rarely stay at the same skill level. Some may have had past lessons and they begin to remember what they previously learned. Also, those who practice more at home progress faster. And, due to learning curve differences, I find that some students "soar" and some "struggle." This is not an issue to me because my goal is that all class members learn the concepts. The number of pieces they learn to play is their choice. Some will learn every piece in the module hands-together. Some will learn fewer pieces and some choose to play their pieces hands-separately.

4. **How do I pace a class so that it meets the needs of varying skill levels?**

   I explain at the first class of each enrollment period that the "train of knowledge" leaves the station that very day and steadily progresses. Gradually moving forward is preferable to teaching to the fastest or slowest student. I also remind students that trains can slow down and/or speed up. It is okay if my lesson plan extends into the next week, because learning to play the piano is a process (not a race). Learning to read the body language of a class helps me to know when the train needs to adjust its speed. Also, once the class members are comfortable with me and each other, they are quite willing to let me know verbally or non-verbally (glazed eyes, frowns, sighs, etc.) that I should consider adjusting the pace. I am not concerned if a student wants to repeat a level to become more secure.

5. **Why do my lesson plans include a Hear-Do-See-Label approach?**

   My goal with each concept or each new piece of music is to make it as easy as I possibly can. Although my RMM classes do not include formal ear-training exercises, I always ask students to make determinations about the sounds they are hearing before they look at the music. After the class has experienced sounds from the new piece, we do activities that prepare them to more easily play what they see when we look at the music. It is helpful to separate sounds and tactile activities from sight.

When we look at the music, we discuss how the piece is organized and add necessary labels. I remind myself to limit the discussion and avoid TMI (too much information). An RMM class is not a theory class, but theoretical concepts can make a piece easier to learn and I do include them in my lesson plan.

6. **Are RMM classes only taught on piano labs?**

My preference is to teach with two pianos side-by-side (one acoustic and one digital). The students are seated in a semi-circle and I rotate them at the pianos. Those not at the pianos are playing on plastic keyboards on their laps, counting aloud, singing or saying note names or finger numbers, etc. Every student should be engaged on every activity. I chose this two-piano arrangement because most public facilities or home studios have at least one piano and arrangements can be made to add an additional piano. Although a class can be taught on two acoustic pianos or two digital pianos, I prefer at least one digital so that I can use MIDI accompaniments and utilize other features of digital pianos in class.

Teachers who prefer to teach on piano labs have the advantage of large ensemble experiences, as well as periodically using headsets for individual practice. A cautionary note, though, is to limit the amount of time spent on headsets. Whether, it's a two-piano setting or a piano lab, avoid the temptation of turning the RMM class into mini-private lessons. It is the "kiss of death" for group learning.

7. **As RMM teaching has the reputation of being stress-free, how is that environment created?**

I begin with the understanding that RMM classes are designed with a focus on student goals rather than teacher goals. RMM students typically want to learn how to read music and to play pieces of their choice. Additionally, they also want to learn to play lead sheets with chords. The underlying foundation of this experience is that it will be non-stressful. RMM classes have the unique challenge of offering quality learning experiences in an atmosphere of fun and enjoyment. I have found humor to be the most successful tool I know. As long as it is not hurtful or directed toward an individual, it tends to dissolve stress quicker than anything I have used.

I try to always remember that many of these students have always yearned to play piano or regretted quitting lessons in the past. RMM learning is a "dream-fulfillment" opportunity and I feel honored to get to partner in anyone's dream. I remind students that there is no expiration date on dreams. Also, I am pleased to report that creating a non-stressful learning environment for students also creates one for me.

8. **Do RMM students perform?**

I leave that decision to individual students. Since solo playing in my classes is voluntary, so is performing in other arenas. Some adults have had past traumatic performance experiences and they quickly communicate they do not want to perform. Others thrive on it and take advantage of every opportunity to do so. Although I do not have recitals, I find an RMM Player's Club to be a fun alternative. Students who hesitate to perform solos often enjoy performing duets. No matter the venue (piano parties, celebrations, etc.) the operative word is "voluntary." As long as it is a non-stressful experience, adults are more inclined to reap the benefits that performance can bring.

9. **Are there resources available for potential RMM teachers?**

RMM Four-DVD Set
On behalf of the National Piano Foundation, sessions at the 2007 MTNA conference were filmed and produced as a four-DVD set. Among the topics are "Getting Started," "Three Different Paths to RMM Teaching," "Partnering with Retailers," etc. Contact the National Piano Foundation at 972/233- 9107 (Ext. 212) to order.

Recreational Music Making Handbook for Piano Teachers
Co-authored by Brian Chung and Brenda Dillon and published by Alfred, this handbook provides a practical, step-by-step foundation for piano teachers who want to develop a program and begin teaching RMM. Topics include "The Philosophy of RMM," "Traditional Versus Recreational Teaching," "Getting Started," "Next Steps," "Principles of Group Teaching," "RMM Teaching on Two Pianos," "RMM Teaching on a Piano Lab," "Lesson Planning" and "Partnering with Retailers." Visit the handbook website for more information, including how to order (www.rmmhandbook.com).

10. **What RMM materials are available after completion of *Piano Fun for Adult Beginners*?**

After a class completes this book, I play pieces from books of diverse styles that are appropriate for the next skill level. Each class votes on the book (or books) they prefer for their next learning challenge. I do require everyone to use the same materials because I learned that letting students bring other books to class has the potential to become a mini-private lesson. We are fortunate to have access to a wealth of published music of diverse styles at different skill levels. For a list of suggested materials, contact Brenda Dillon at brenda@dondillon.com or her website (www.brendadillon.com).

Glossary of Musical Terms and Symbols

ACCIDENTALS:

♭   **Flat sign** – Play the next key to the left, whether it's black or white.

♯   **Sharp sign** – Play the next key to the right, black or white.

♮   **Natural sign** – Cancels a flat or a sharp.

ARTICULATION MARKS:

Staccato – Play the note shorter than notated, usually half the value.

Accent – Play the note louder.

Fermata – Hold the note or chord indefinitely.

DYNAMICS:

pp   **Pianissimo** – Play very soft.

p   **Piano** – Play soft.

mp   **Mezzo-piano** – Play half as soft as piano.

mf   **Mezzo-forte** – Play half as loud as forte.

f   **Forte** – Play loud.

ff   **Fortissimo** – Play very loud.

Crescendo – Gradually increase the volume.

Decrescendo – Gradually decrease the volume.

NOTE RELATIONSHIPS:

 Tie – a curved line connecting two notes on the same line or space which is held for the combined value of both notes

 **Slur** – a curved line over or under different notes that are to be played smoothly (legato)

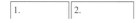 **Phrase** – a musical thought indicated by a slur

REPETITION AND CODAS:

‖: :‖ **Repeat signs** – Play the section more than once. If there is no left repeat sign, go back to the beginning or to the nearest double bar.

|1. |2. **First and second endings** – After playing the first ending, repeat the designated section and jump to the second ending.

D.C. al Fine **Da Capo al Fine** – Repeat the song from the beginning and play to fine and stop.

D.S. al Coda **Dal segno al Coda** – Repeat from the sign (𝄋) to the coda sign (⊕).

TEMPO (RATE OF SPEED):

Adagio – slow

Andante – walking speed (relaxed)

Moderato – moderate speed

Allegro – a lively speed

Vivace – quick

Ritardando (Rit.) – gradually slow down

A tempo – resume original speed

OTHER:

Half step – the distance from one key to the next closest key up or down on the keyboard

Key signature – sharps or flats that appear at the beginning of each line of music

Metronome – a rhythm device that ticks a steady beat and can be adjusted slower or faster

Octave – the interval of eight letter names between two notes of the same name

Whole step – two half steps up or down on the keyboard

Hal Leonard Student Piano Library

Adult Piano Method

Adult Piano Method

Adults want to play rewarding music and enjoy their piano study. They deserve a method that lives up to those expectations. The *Hal Leonard Student Piano Library Adult Piano Method* does just that and more.

Method Book 1
00296441 Book/Online Audio $16.99

Method Book 2
00296480 Book/Online Audio $16.99

Popular Hits Book 1

Our hit-packed supplementary songbook includes these titles: American Pie • Circle of Life • Fun, Fun, Fun • Let It Be Me • Murder, She Wrote • The Music of the Night • My Heart Will Go On • Sing • Strangers in the Night • Vincent (Starry Starry Night) • Y.M.C.A. • The Way You Look Tonight.
00296541 Book/Online Audio $14.99

Popular Hits Book 2

12 hits: I Will Remember You • I Wish You Love • I Write the Songs • In the Mood • Moon River • Oh, Pretty Woman • The Phantom of the Opera • Stand by Me • Tears in Heaven • Unchained Melody • What a Wonderful World • When I'm Sixty-Four.
00296652 Book/Online Audio $12.99

Popular Favorites Book 1

11 favorites: Are You Lonesome Tonight? • Bless the Broken Road • Don't Know Why • Every Breath You Take • From a Distance • Help Me Make It Through the Night • I Hope You Dance • Imagine • Lean on Me • The Nearness of You • Right Here Waiting.
00296826 Book/Enhanced CD Pack...$12.99

Popular Favorites Book 2

12 classics: All I Have to Do Is Dream • Georgia on My Mind • I Just Called to Say I Love You • I'm a Believer • Memory • Never on a Sunday • On My Own • One Fine Day • Satin Doll • That'll Be the Day • We Are the World • Your Song.
00296842 Book/Enhanced CD Pack...$12.99

Christmas Favorites Book 1

12 favorites: Away in a Manger • Deck the Hall • God Rest Ye Merry, Gentlemen • I Saw Three Ships • Jingle Bells • Joy to the World • O Come, O Come, Emmanuel • O Little Town of Bethleham • Silent Night • Ukrainian Bell Carol • We Wish You a Merry Christmas • What Child Is This?
00296544 Book/Online Audio $12.99

Christmas Favorites Book 2

12 more holiday classics: Angels We Have Heard on High • Bring a Torch, Jeannette Isabella • Dance of the Sugar Plum Fairy • Ding Dong! Merrily on High! • The First Noel • Go, Tell It on the Mountain • Hark! The Herald Angels Sing • The Holly and the Ivy • O Christmas Tree • O Holy Night • Still, Still, Still • We Three Kings of Orient Are.
00296668 Book/Online Audio $12.99

Traditional Hymns Book 1

16 sacred favorites: All Glory, Laud and Honor • Come, Thou Almighty King • For the Beauty of the Earth • Holy, Holy, Holy! • It Is Well with My Soul • Joyful, Joyful, We Adore Thee • A Mighty Fortress Is Our God • What a Friend We Have in Jesus • and more.
00296782 Book/CD Pack...$12.99

Traditional Hymns Book 2

15 more traditional hymns: All Things Bright and Beautiful • Ezekiel Saw the Wheel • God of Grace and God of Glory • God Will Take Care of You • In the Garden • Lord, I Want to Be a Christian • Stand Up, Stand Up for Jesus • Swing Low, Sweet Chariot • This Is My Father's World • and more.
00296783 Book/CD Pack...$12.99

Prices, contents and availability are subject to change without notice.

www.halleonard.com